21 Days of Prayer and Fasting

Revised and Expanded
Second Edition

J. Randolph Turpin, Jr.

21 Days of Prayer and Fasting

Revised and Expanded
Second Edition

J. Randolph Turpin, Jr.

DECLARATION PRESS

21 DAYS OF PRAYER AND FASTING, second edition
By J. Randolph Turpin, Jr.

Original text copyright © 2016 by J. Randolph Turpin, Jr.
Second edition copyright © 2024 by J. Randolph Turpin, Jr.

All rights reserved. No portion of this book may be reproduced, stored in a retrieval system, or transmitted in any form or by any means—electronic, mechanical, photocopy, recording, scanning, or other—except for brief quotations in critical reviews or articles, without the prior written permission of the author.

Scripture taken from the Holy Bible, New International Version®, NIV®. Copyright © 1973, 1978, 1984, 2011 by Biblica, Inc.™ Used by permission of Zondervan. All rights reserved worldwide. The "NIV" and "New International Version" are trademarks registered in the United States Patent and Trademark Office by Biblica, Inc.™

Scripture taken from the Modern English Version®, MEV®. Copyright © 2014 by Military Bible Association. Used by permission. All rights reserved.

Published by Declaration Press

Declaration Press
P.O. Box 680392
Franklin, TN 37068

ISBN: 979-8-9891257-3-9

Important Health Notice: Before beginning any fast, particularly an extended one, please consult your physician. This is especially important if you have existing health conditions. Some individuals should not fast for medical reasons. The information in this book is not intended to replace professional medical advice.

Please note that this twenty-one-day period of prayer and fasting does not require everyone to fast for twenty-one consecutive days. Rather, it represents a season of spiritual emphasis where individuals voluntarily choose their own level of participation and type of fasting according to their personal circumstances and convictions. Some may fast for the full period, while others may fast intermittently or in different ways throughout these twenty-one days.

Contents

Preface	1
Introduction	7
1. What Is Fasting?	11
2. Why Fast?	13
3. Why Pray?	23
4. Things that Nullify Fasting	31
5. How to Fast	35
6. Congregational Implementation	49
Conclusion	63
21-Day Journal	65

Preface

Preface to the 2025 Edition

I am writing these words in the quiet stillness of Christmas morning, 2024, while the rest of my household sleeps. There's an unmistakable stirring in my spirit—a deep conviction that we stand at the threshold of something momentous in God's timeline. The church is being drawn into a season of profound repentance and purification, a divine invitation to humble ourselves before the Lord. If there has ever been a time when God's people needed to fast and pray, it is now.

As my wife Kerry and I began preparing the audio edition of the 2016 version of this book, it became increasingly clear that the manuscript needed more than just a technical update. The spiritual landscape has shifted significantly since the first edition. There is a palpable change in the spiritual atmosphere—a sense that our nation is entering the early stages of what many believe could be the next great spiritual awakening. This awareness compelled us to pause the audiobook project and undertake a more comprehensive revision that would serve the church more effectively in this critical hour.

This new edition expands significantly on the original work, addressing the unique challenges and opportunities of seeking God through fasting and prayer in our modern context. I've added practical guidance on digital fasting—a crucial discipline in our technology-saturated age. I've also incorporated new content dealing with navigating fasting and prayer within family life—including the particular challenges faced by parents.

Additionally, the book addresses the complexities of maintaining a fasting lifestyle in contemporary work environments, recognizing that many believers struggle to integrate spiritual disciplines with professional demands.

Acknowledging the holistic nature of our walk with God, we've included new material on fasting in relation to mental health and stress management. We've expanded our exploration of different types of fasting, providing more detailed guidance for those seeking to discover the approach best suited to their situation.

To strengthen content dealing with congregational implementation, comprehensive guidelines for conducting a solemn assembly are included—a timely addition as more congregations feel called to corporate seasons of seeking God.

At the end of this paperback edition, you'll find a section for twenty-one days of journaling—space to document your insights, prayers, and experiences as you undertake this spiritual journey. I encourage you to use these pages to record what God reveals to you during your season of prayer and fasting.

The decision to release this edition in the opening days of 2025 feels divinely timed. While only time will reveal the full scope of what God is doing in our day, I am convinced that those who position themselves through prayer and fasting will witness and participate in extraordinary movements of his Spirit. My prayer is that this expanded edition will serve as a practical guide and source of inspiration as you seek to enter more fully into what God is doing in our time.

May God use these pages to draw you deeper into his presence and purpose.

J. Randolph Turpin, Jr.
Christmas Day, 2024

Preface to the 2016 Edition

In the early 1990s, I served as a pastor in Windham, Maine. At that time, many Christians felt drawn to extended prayer and fasting, and so did I. During this season of my life, I started fasting for the first three weeks of each year.

I learned that fasting is most productive when initiated or led by the Holy Spirit. I would often ask him for guidance before entering a fast. As a result, the Spirit led me to fast for twenty-one days every January. These spiritual encounters began several years before three-week Daniel fasts became popular.

Across America, the church was hungry for God. After several years of disillusionment in the late 1980s, there was a general sense that there just had to be more to this Christian life than most of us were experiencing. Then, in the mid-to-late 1990s, the breakthroughs came. God heard our cry, and times of refreshing came to the church in many parts of the world, including our region in Southern Maine.

While continuing in the River of Revival, we sustained our emphasis on prayer and fasting as we entered the new century. Initially, I did not connect our twenty-one-day emphasis with the twenty-one-day fast in the tenth chapter of Daniel. My decision to mark off twenty-one days was a pragmatic choice. A twenty-one-day stretch was reachable, and it was a reasonable number of days for leading a congregation into a corporate experience of consecration to God.

Since those early pastoral years, I have led five congregations in the twenty-one-day journey. I have also presented this model to countless others in seminars, conferences, my "Developing Congregational Prayer Ministries" course at the Pentecostal Theological Seminary, and my book *101 Prayer Models*. Several other leaders have acquired my outlines and handouts on this subject and have incorporated the material in their contexts. I do not claim to be the originator of the popular "twenty-one day" model, but some of my ideas have been used in the prayer movement. I make this point only to clarify potential questions regarding sources and originality. All glory belongs to God, for the Holy Spirit conceived the twenty-one-day model in the hearts of many who were yearning for a move of God in the 1990's.

Several people have impacted my life in the areas of prayer, fasting, and personal spirituality. Some are individuals with whom I have had little personal contact, yet they have been an influence from a distance—such as Larry Lea and David Yonggi Cho. Literary influences include the works of Andrew Murray and Beni Johnson of Bethel Church in Redding, California. Others with whom I have been more personally involved include Douglas Small, Kathy Hamon, and Steve Backlund of Bethel Church in Redding, California. Yet others have been personal mentors in prayer—people like Pastor Calvin Rogers, Pastor J. D. Simmons, and my parents, Jim and Betty Turpin. By crediting the influence of these people on my life, I am crediting their indirect impact on the preparation of this material.

I hope this succinct guide continues benefiting individuals and congregations aspiring to be prayerful. For some, it may prove to be one component among many contributing to new initiatives in spiritual renewal. However you choose to use this resource, may it draw you and others into a deeper walk with Christ.

J. Randolph Turpin, Jr.
December 19, 2016

Introduction

For twenty-one days, the prophet Daniel fasted to gain understanding and to humble himself before God. He ate no meat, and he drank no wine. At the end of the twenty-one days, a glorious celestial being appeared to him, saying,

> "Do not be afraid, Daniel. Since the first day that you set your mind to gain understanding and to humble yourself before your God, your words were heard, and I have come in response to them. But the prince of the Persian kingdom resisted me twenty-one days. Then Michael, one of the chief princes, came to help me, because I was detained there with the king of Persia. Now I have come to explain to you what will happen to your people in the future, for the vision concerns a time yet to come" (Daniel 10:12–14 (NIV).

Daniel had fasted and prayed for three weeks, but the answer to his prayer had been hindered in the spirit realm by an entity known as "the prince of the Persian kingdom." Although it may have appeared that heaven was not responding, a breakthrough came at the end of Daniel's fast, and his prayer was answered.

In an earlier account in the first chapter of Daniel, the story is told of four young Hebrews who had been recruited for training in the service of Nebuchadnezzar, king of Babylon. Daniel was one of the young men. When portions of food and wine were assigned to them from the king's table, they asked for permission not to defile themselves by partaking of this provision. To prove to the chief official that they could be sustained without eating the king's meat, they ate only vegetables and drank water for ten days. At the end of ten days, they were healthier than any of the other trainees. From that point forward, they were allowed to abstain from eating the king's food and continued gaining favor in his eyes.

Many have drawn inspiration and instruction from these two stories to guide their own fasting practices. Daniel's practice of limiting his diet to vegetables and abstaining from choice foods—meat and wine—has become known as the "Daniel fast." His twenty-one-day fast in Daniel 10 is the biblical precedent for the twenty-one-day pattern many have chosen to follow.

Cultivating a Prayer Culture

Fasting and praying for twenty-one days is not an end in itself. One reason congregational leaders follow the twenty-one-day model is to introduce (or, in some cases, re-introduce) the church to the ongoing disciplines of prayer and fasting. The objective is to provide an opportunity for the Holy Spirit to create a love and hunger for a lifestyle of prayer and intimate communion with God. The ultimate aim is cultivating and sustaining a culture of prayer among God's people.

The emphasis on prayer and fasting, as set forth here, is one part of a more extensive prayer culture training experience. Other components include the cultivation of intercessory mindsets and the introduction of multiple and varied prayer models. This prayer culture model has been tested in several ministry contexts. When implemented in New England, participants became instrumental in affecting a measure of revival in their congregation. When implemented in Florida, the people transitioned from a clergy-driven to more of a lay-driven ministry. Whereas previously, the pastor of that particular church had been the "anointed man of God" (i.e., the one that God worked through to do supernatural things), the church members soon became the Lord's instruments through whom signs and wonders were performed. When this plan was implemented in yet another church in Minnesota, it was partly responsible for propelling the people into what became a prayer movement.

As you embark on this twenty-one-day journey, do so with an expectation that you and your church will encounter God more deeply. Allow the cultivation of an intercessory mindset to take place in your life. Embrace the belief that God wants to perform great and mighty things through your prayers and obedient service. A great awakening is about to begin with *you*.

1

What Is Fasting?

SOMETIMES, TO BETTER UNDERSTAND what something is, it is helpful to understand what it is not. As Edwin Louis Cole used to say, "Fasting is *not* a hunger strike." It is not a way to strengthen your demand, saying, "God, I'm not going to eat until you answer this prayer!" Fasting is *not* an attempt to manipulate God or to force his hand. It is *not* a way to place demands upon God, forcing him to submit to your desires and answer your prayers.

Neither is fasting an attempt to get God to love you more. He already loves you more than you could ever comprehend. Before you do anything of a spiritual nature, he loves you. What we need is to have hearts that are open to how great his love truly is. If anything needs to change, it is not the greatness of his love toward us. What might need to change is the capacity of our hearts to receive his love. Know that he is already gracious toward you. He already wants to answer your prayers.

Fasting also has nothing to do with salvation. Some reading this material may be struggling with sin or some area of bondage. Fasting *can* help bring a person to a place of personal freedom, but it is not to be viewed as a type of extreme sacrifice that you can make that will pay for your sins. God does not require that of you. He *does not need* to require that of you. *Jesus*

Christ has paid the full price for your salvation. Nothing more needs to be paid. When we get to heaven, God will not line us up and say, "Everybody who has gone through a forty-day fast, stand over here, and everybody who has gone through a twenty-one-day fast, stand over there." No, fasting has nothing to do with some way that God might classify you. That is not the way he sees you.

What then is fasting? Somewhere along the way, I picked up this definition of fasting: to voluntarily deprive oneself of physical nourishment in order to accomplish a spiritual purpose.

Old and New Testament Fasting

Our aim is to comprehend fasting from a New Testament perspective, but it is informative to know how the practice was understood in the Old Testament. The Old and New Covenants have similarities and contrasts.

In the Old Testament, fasting was associated with humbling the soul. In a time when David's *enemies* were ill, he interceded for them and humbled himself with fasting. In Psalm 35:13, he sang, "I put on sackcloth and humbled myself with fasting." So, fasting is one of the ways that we can humble ourselves before the Lord.

The purpose of fasting in the Old Testament was to mortify oneself—putting to death fleshly desires. It was about self-renunciation. It was often even associated with mourning (Joel 2:12). Under the New Testament, fasting still relates to humility and subduing the flesh, and when it is practiced along with repentance, one will still experience sorrow for sins. However, that sorrow will be short-lived. Under the new covenant, joy overshadows sorrow once the heart has turned to God. Generally, New Testament fasting is characterized by joy, not sorrow.

2

Why Fast?

It is important to understand why we fast, just as it is important to know why we do anything in the Christian walk. If we do not comprehend the "why" or the purpose, we will not likely sustain the practice, especially when it becomes difficult. If you do not understand the purpose of fasting, you will get two or three days into the fast, and your hunger will force you to ask, "Why? Why am I doing this? Why am I putting myself through this?" When you understand why you are fasting, you will persevere through the difficult points of the fast, knowing that it is worth it.

Someone has spoken in these terms concerning the purpose of both prayer and fasting: "With prayer, we lay hold of the heavenly. With fasting, we cast aside the earthly" (author unknown). Fasting and prayer go hand in hand.

The purpose of fasting relates almost entirely to the good that the practice accomplishes in our lives, and the benefits of fasting are many. Let us now consider in greater detail the multiple purposes of fasting:

1. To assist us in turning to God with the whole heart. Fasting assists us in putting God first above food, friends, amusements, etc. In Joel

2:12, the Lord said, "Return to me with all your heart, with fasting and weeping and mourning."

There are times when some weeping and mourning may be appropriate while fasting, especially when repentance is involved. We may be repenting over our own sins, or we may be repenting for the sins of our nation. In those times, some tears are needed. However, as New Testament believers, our lives are to be centered on God's presence, and in his presence, there is fullness of *joy* (Psalm 16:11). Jesus taught us to anoint ourselves with oil and to put on a joyful countenance when we fast (Matthew 6:16–18).

2. To humble ourselves before God. As already noted, fasting is a way to do this. When we fast, we are not fasting *for* ourselves. We are totally *removing* ourselves from the picture. Fasting is not me-centered.

Two promises accompany humbling ourselves before the Lord, and they are found in the book of James. First, God gives *grace* to the humble. In James 4:6, we are told, "God opposes the proud, but He gives grace to the humble." The "grace" element in this verse is the part that catches our attention, but let us not run too swiftly past the issue of "pride."

Do you ever feel like God is working against you? In most cases, it is probably the devil and not God who is working against you, but sometimes we do need to consider this possibility: "God opposes the proud." Pride has to do with us thinking of ourselves more highly than we ought to think. It is a feeling of superiority—not just a sense of being better than others but also an attitude of being above the need to change. None of us like to think that God might oppose us, but he will oppose us if we operate in pride. We often do not recognize our sin of pride until the Lord shines some light on it. Fasting is a good way to open our hearts for the Holy Spirit to reveal areas of pride. If and when he reveals pride in your heart, humble yourself, confess it as sin, repent, and receive forgiveness. Recognizing and eliminating pride is a key to entering God's best for your life.

James said, "God gives *grace* to the humble." If fasting is a way to humble ourselves before God, then it follows that grace comes upon us in our times of fasting. What is grace? Grace is favor, but it is more. What is God's favor? God's favor is his face shining upon us. When his face shines upon us, he is manifesting his presence. Grace is God's presence in our lives. Grace is his power and his anointing. If you carefully study the theme of "grace" in the New Testament, you will find that it is often connected with the presence and work of the Holy Spirit. When God's grace is at work, his Spirit is at work.

I want to say a little more about understanding grace as *favor*. We most often appreciate this favor in terms of our salvation and our acceptance into God's family, but do we also realize that it can affect every aspect of our lives? When we experience God's favor, doors open, obstacles are removed, and wisdom is given so we might live the wonderful life our Father intended us to live. May the revelation of this favor overtake us.

Second, when we humble ourselves, God will lift us up. James 4:10 says, "Humble yourselves in the sight of the Lord, and He will lift you up." God wants to lift us, not only to bring us into a new realm of blessing but also to elevate us to a new place of influence. However, **we** are not to elevate ourselves. Elevation or exaltation is something that **God** will do in our lives when we walk in humility. Humbling ourselves through fasting prepares us for promotion.

It is so important how we enter and leave opportunities and life seasons. I have occasionally heard Bill Johnson and others say we should always enter "low." We should not enter any situation thinking, "I deserve this or that." Instead, we should enter thinking, "Anything good that I may receive from this opportunity is only by the goodness of God."

My wife, Kerry, often uses this illustration. There are two ways to enter a room. We can enter a room saying, "Here I am, everybody!" or we can enter saying, "There *you* are!" The first shows evidence of pride, and the second testifies of humility. The Bible says, "In humility, value others above yourselves" (Philippians 2:3). When we elevate others above ourselves, we have, in effect, made ourselves lower. We are talking about following the example of Jesus in taking the nature of a servant (Philippians 2:7). When the Lord sees such a heart in a man or woman, he is willing to entrust promotion to that person.

Fasting is a means for arriving at this place of humility. Once we get beyond our awareness of hunger, which usually happens after the third day of a fast, we begin to think less of ourselves and become more aware of God. Fasting heightens a person's awareness of God. When we become more aware of him, we start sensing his heart toward others, and when we are in touch with his affections, the concerns of others often become more important than our own.

3. To identify with Jesus's life and mission and prepare us for greater works. Jesus fasted. If he did it, we want to do it! Fasting is part of following him. It is part of following him into the wilderness. Jesus fasted forty days in the wilderness in preparation for a great work (Matthew 4:1–11).

Jesus taught us to expect greater works—even miracles—through our lives. He said,

> "Very truly I tell you, whoever believes in me will do the works I have been doing, and they will do even greater things than these, because I am going to the Father" (John 14:12).

In God's kingdom, the path to greatness always involves humility. When Jesus humbled himself through fasting, he was preparing for a ministry of signs, wonders, and miracles. We are invited to do the same. To learn more about the role of humility, reflect on Matthew 20:26, John 13:1–17, and Philippians 2:1–11

4. To put priorities in proper order. When we fast, we prioritize hearing God's voice over our own physical nourishment. In Matthew 4:4, Jesus said, "Man does not live on bread alone, but on every word that comes from the mouth of God."

These words from our Lord are, in part, about setting priorities. Our priority should be that we do not live solely by temporal means. We will not live the life that Jesus has for us as long as we are preoccupied with the temporal: "bread alone." We are to live on "every word that comes from the mouth of God." We live for what he has to say to us.

God wants you to *feast* while you are fasting! Crave for every word you can receive from the mouth of God. Everything that he says is life-giving, whether it comes through the Bible or prophetic illumination. Have an appetite that says, "I don't want to miss a thing that he has to say!" When you are fasting, *you are creating a void* in your life. Fill that void with the word of God.

5. To remove unbelief and to establish us in spiritual authority. In Matthew 17:19–21 and Mark 9:14–29, the story is told of the inability of Jesus' disciples to cast a demon out of a boy. When they asked him why they could not deliver the child, Jesus told them it was because of their unbelief. Then, according to the Modern English Version and King James Version rendering of this account, Jesus said, "This kind does not go out except by prayer and fasting." The implication is that fasting counters unbelief. When one considers that fasting is, in a sense, an extreme act of trust or faith, its power over unbelief makes sense.

Fasting is also an act of submitting oneself to God's authority. We gain authority over dark spiritual forces when we submit to *God's* authority. Our power over those forces is based on the alignment of our lives with

God's rule. Fasting positions us as agents authorized to execute and enforce the work of God's kingdom.

6. To prepare us for hearing God's voice. On one occasion, when the church at Antioch was "worshiping the Lord and fasting," they heard the Holy Spirit speak to them, calling for the commissioning of Barnabas and Saul (Acts 13:2). Fasting heightens spiritual sensitivities, increasing the likelihood that the Spirit's voice will be heard. Note that in the Antioch scenario, the entire church community was worshiping and fasting. As a result, the whole congregation was activated as a prophetic community. A community-wide consensus was reached because there was a general sense that God was indeed speaking.

7. To prepare us for a missional shift. This point is an extension of the preceding one related to hearing God's voice. A shift in mission requires a new mandate or directive from heaven. Awareness of that directive requires divine guidance. The Antioch scenario is an ideal example. As a result of the congregation's shared discernment, Barnabas and Saul's mission to the Gentile world was initiated. When a shift in mission is anticipated, fasting prepares us for moving with the Spirit in the transition.

8. To seek the Lord's manifest presence—to become more aware of and passionate for him. While Jesus was still among his disciples, there was no need for them to hunger for his presence because he was already constantly with them. He anticipated a time when he would no longer be physically present with his disciples. When that time would come, they would miss him and desire his manifest presence. In reference to their desire for him, Jesus said, "The time will come when the bridegroom will be taken from them; then they will fast" (Matthew 9:15).

Now that Jesus is no longer physically present with us, we yearn for his presence. We hunger for him. We cannot wait to see him face-to-face. Out of our love and passion for him, we fast. Bodily appetites can distract us from the awareness of God's Presence. Fasting helps us fine-tune that awareness.

When on an extended fast (more than three days), at the beginning of the fast, you are fasting so that you might become more aware of him. Initially, your hunger may actually make you more aware of yourself! We say to ourselves, "I thought this was about me getting closer to God, but all I can do is think about how hungry I am! I am just more aware of *me* right now and how miserable I am!"

Initially, all this fleshly stuff comes to the surface—not just cravings for food. We become aware of our rotten attitudes and unconfessed sins. What are we to do? Just bring it to the Lord. Confess, repent, and receive his forgiveness. However, as the fast progresses, something amazing usually happens. You can become so aware of him that you cease to be so aware of your fleshly junk. You can even reach a point where physical food no longer matters because of your awareness of God. Jesus promised, "Blessed are those who hunger and thirst for righteousness, for they will be filled" (Matthew 5:6).

9. To bring the body into subjection to the Spirit and the Word, assisting in our pursuit of self-control and discipline. The Apostle Paul worked to keep his body under subjection so that he might not be disqualified from receiving the benefits of the grace he preached (1 Corinthians 9:27). Fasting helps to crucify carnal desires. In Romans 13:14, Paul said, "Clothe yourselves with the Lord Jesus Christ, and do not think about how to gratify the desires of the flesh." The King James Version rendering of these words emphasizes that believers are to make no provision for the flesh. Fasting helps to remove patterns of thought and conduct that support fleshly and undisciplined behavior.

10. To become men and women of tears. I am reminded of when the report came from Judah to Nehemiah about the condition of Jerusalem.

How did Nehemiah respond? In his own words, Nehemiah recorded, "When I heard these things, I sat down and wept. For some days I mourned and fasted and prayed before the God of heaven" (Nehemiah 1:4).

As noted earlier, it is appropriate to weep and mourn over some things during a fast, but we are not to *stay* indefinitely in that place of grief. How are we to regulate these emotions? It is a good idea to ask the Father to give us his heart during a fast. Say to him, "Lord, I want you to break my heart with the things that are breaking your heart." If the Father is feeling joy over something, then I want to be rejoicing, but if he is grieved, then I want to feel his grief and conduct myself accordingly.

11. To make ourselves weak so that we might know his strength. God's strength shows itself to be most effective in our times of weakness. In fasting, we join the Apostle Paul, saying, "When I am weak, then I am strong (2 Corinthians 12:9–10). Depriving ourselves of physical nourishment helps us to reach a point of total reliance on God. Through fasting, our attitude tells the Lord, "It's you or nothing!" When we fast, we realize that apart from whatever God may provide, we have nothing to offer him. Our resources are insufficient. We come to the realization that *he* is our sufficiency.

Digital Fasting in the Modern Age

In our hyper-connected world, many believers are discovering the value of digital fasting—temporarily abstaining from social media, entertainment streaming, gaming, or other forms of digital consumption. This practice can powerfully complement traditional food fasting or serve as an alternative for those who cannot fast from food for medical reasons.

Benefits of Digital Fasting

Digital fasting serves several spiritual purposes:

1. Mental clarity and focus. Constant digital connectivity can fragment our attention and create mental noise that interferes with hearing God's voice. Temporarily disconnecting from these inputs can create mental space for deeper communion with God.

2. Time stewardship. The hours usually spent scrolling social media or streaming entertainment can be redirected to prayer, Bible study, and ministry. People are surprised to discover how much time becomes available when they fast from digital distractions.

3. Heart examination. Digital fasting often reveals unhealthy dependencies or attachments we've developed to social media validation, entertainment, or digital distraction. This awareness can lead to beneficial lifestyle adjustments extending beyond fasting.

4. Enhanced presence. Stepping away from screens can help us become more present to God, our families, and others around us. Many report experiencing deeper relationships and more meaningful conversations during digital fasts.

Practical Approaches to Digital Fasting

Practical approaches to digital fasting might include:

- Complete disconnection from social media platforms,

- Limiting smartphone use to essential communications only,

- Abstaining from streaming entertainment services,

- Taking breaks from news consumption and internet browsing,

- Turning off all notifications except those truly necessary, and

- Restricting email checking to specific times of day.

As with any fast, the goal is not legalistic adherence to rules but creating space for deeper communion with God. Ask the Holy Spirit for guidance on what form of digital fasting would most benefit your spiritual growth.

Whether we fast from food, digital distractions, or both, the underlying spiritual principles remain the same. Every fast is an opportunity to humble ourselves, create space for God, and reset our priorities. Through fasting—in all its forms—we declare that our deepest hunger is not for physical food or worldly connections but for intimacy with God.

3

Why Pray?

SEVERAL YEARS AGO, WHILE preparing to conduct a prayer ministry seminar, I decided to poll my Facebook friends to learn what they thought to be important topics to cover in prayer ministry training. One of the most insightful responses I received came from my son-in-law, Jonathan Zajas, who said,

We should not assume that people know *how* to pray or *why* they should pray. If believers do not grasp the *why* and *how* of prayer, we should not be surprised when they do not consistently pray in a disciplined manner.

If we do not grasp why we pray, we will not be very consistent or persistent with it. It will be one of those activities we let slide, not a priority. Why, then, do we pray? What difference does it make?

1. Prayer glorifies God. Jesus promised, "I will do whatever you ask in my name, so that the Son may bring glory to the Father" (John 14:13).

2. Prayer is where we connect with God in holy friendship. We commune with God in prayer, and we enjoy our time with him. He listens to us, and we listen to him. We give him our hearts, and he gives us his.

3. Prayer accesses divine assistance. Jesus taught us to ask for our daily provision by praying, "Give us today our daily bread" (Matthew 6:11).

4. Prayer is how God gets things done. God works through prayer to accomplish his will.

What Difference Does It Make?

Does prayer really make a difference in what God does? Why bother praying if he is going to do whatever he wants, whether we pray or not? If we do not pray, *will* God just do what he wants to do? No, God does not act apart from involving us. There may be some exceptions, but typically, he accomplishes his purposes on earth in response to the prayers and obedience of human agents.

Jesus taught us to pray, "Your kingdom come, your will be done, on earth as it is in heaven" (Matthew 6:10). How does God's will get done on earth as in heaven? God's will is done when his people do his will and pray his will.

Someone may ask, "Are you suggesting that God is sitting in heaven waiting for us to pray before he performs his acts on earth?"

Yes, that is basically what I am saying. The point might be slightly overstated, but generally speaking, yes—especially concerning his redemptive works on the earth. Dutch Sheets said, "God chose, from the beginning of Creation, to work on the earth through humans, not independent of them" (*Intercessory Prayer*, 29).

Think about it. Throughout Scripture, isn't it true? Consider the time the Hebrews worshipped a golden calf. (You can read about this in Exodus 32.) God decreed judgment. However, Moses prayed. Consequently, God withheld judgment. A petition uttered on the lips of a mere man altered the course of what God would or would not do.

Consider the time when Hezekiah was dying. (That story is in 2 Kings 20 and Isaiah 38.) Hezekiah was, in fact, dying. Isaiah confirmed, "The

Lord says you are going to die; you will not recover." We all know that if God says something will happen, it will happen. If he says something will not happen, it will not happen. So, God said to Hezekiah, "You are going to die, and you are not going to recover."

However, Hezekiah prayed. What happened next? The Lord healed him. Human beings *can* make a difference in what God does on earth simply by praying.

Why do the prayers of us mortal creatures mean so much to God? There is a reason. From the beginning, he authorized humanity to rule in the affairs of earth. In Genesis 1:26–28, God said,

> "Let us make man in our image, in our likeness, and let them rule over the fish of the sea and the birds of the air, over the livestock, over all the earth, and over all the creatures that move along the ground. Be fruitful and increase in number; fill the earth and subdue it. Rule over the fish of the sea and the birds of the air and over every living creature that moves on the ground."

In Psalm 8:3–8, the psalmist said,

> "What is man that you are mindful of him, the son of man that you care for him? You made him a little lower than the heavenly beings and crowned him with glory and honor. You made him ruler over the works of your hands; you put everything under his feet...."

Humans have been appointed to rule the earth, and God will not step around us to accomplish his purposes on the planet. He will not work apart from the authority he has already given us.

So, how does God accomplish what he wants to do on earth? He accomplishes what he wants to do by first revealing his will to us. Then, it is up to us to pray his will and to obey. He *relies* upon us to pray. Through prayer, we, as the appointed authorities over the earth, invite God into the situations of earth to accomplish heaven's purposes.

We cannot afford to be passive in this matter of the will of God. God's will is not just automatically done. Let us think this through. Somewhere today, someone went into eternity without Christ. Was that God's will? Was God's will done in that situation? Of course not. Scripture clearly teaches that it is not his will that any perish (2 Peter 3:9). God has many things he wants to accomplish on earth. He wants to manifest mercy instead of judgment, but he is waiting, even longing, for someone to act or pray on the basis of his will.

Sometimes people will pray a prayer, and the prayer is not answered. Some are too quick to make this assumption: "It must not have been God's will." Others conclude that God's will cannot be known. The truth is that God delights in revealing his will to his people. When he reveals it, we are to act upon it, pray it, and settle for nothing less than his will being done.

The line in the prayer Jesus taught us in Matthew 6:10, "Your will be done," is not just some blanket statement that we thoughtlessly throw on top of our prayers. No, we are to find out what his will is—what pleases the Lord—and then we are to pray that thing or do that thing.

Are there instances of God acting redemptively without someone praying? That is not likely. Prayer is almost always required. While it may appear that God has, at times, worked without anyone praying, it is more likely that he did indeed call upon someone to pray, and we didn't know about it.

Allow me to demonstrate how this works with a hypothetical example. A single mother in North Carolina has a young child with a fever. She is not a woman of prayer, and she does not have anyone in her life who knows how to pray. God, in his compassion, wants to heal the child, so he causes his Holy Spirit to move upon an available intercessor on the other side of the planet in Mongolia. The intercessor prays in the Spirit for twenty minutes or more, not knowing for whom he is praying. Suddenly, the child's fever breaks. Only heaven knows how this breakthrough has been arranged, but it involved the critical role of an available and willing intercessor on the earth. I would like to think that there are entire congregations that have made themselves available to pray in such a way.

Something similar happened to me during my college years. One evening, as I walked from the cafeteria toward my dorm, I felt an unmistakable pull from the Holy Spirit directing me to the campus prayer rooms. The moment my knees touched the floor, a powerful spirit of intercession descended upon me. For the next hour, no words passed my lips—only deep, intense groanings emerged from my soul. I believe I was experiencing exactly what the Apostle Paul described in Romans 8:26, where the Spirit intercedes through us with groanings too deep for words. The intensity of this prayer was so profound that my clothes became drenched with perspiration as I groaned in fervent intercession for an unknown cause or person. When the burden of prayer suddenly lifted, an overwhelming peace flooded my being. Whatever heavenly transaction had taken place was now complete.

To this day, I remain unaware of what or who I was praying for, but I am certain of this: somewhere on earth, God needed something accomplished, and He spotted a simple college student walking to his dorm. He chose to work through that young man to align earthly circumstances with heavenly purposes—to ensure his will would be done on earth as it is in heaven.

A Few Testimonies of Answered Prayer

As you can see, these principles are not mere theory—they are demonstrated through countless answered prayers. Let me share just a few other examples from my own journey of seeing God work through prayer.

As a junior high student, I witnessed the transforming power of persistent intercession. Classmates who had once mocked my faith became fervent followers of Jesus after I committed to praying for them daily after school. This early experience taught me that seemingly impossible situations can change through faithful prayer.

Sometimes, God answers prayer in surprisingly specific ways. During college, I struggled with a malfunctioning watch that consistently made me late for classes. One day in my dorm room, I simply prayed, "Lord, I need you to fix this watch or get me a new one." From that moment, the watch began keeping perfect time, allowing me to meet every appointment punctually. Months later, when my parents gave me a new watch for Christmas, I noticed that the old one immediately stopped working—as if it had been supernaturally sustained just long enough to meet my need.

Prayer can also bring breakthrough in seemingly impossible financial situations. While serving as a Christian school administrator, we faced a severe budget crisis that threatened to close our doors. Walking into the post office one day to check the school's mail, I prayed, "God, you are our provider, and I know that you can reach back in time and place it on somebody's heart to send us what we need to make budget." Opening the mailbox, I found a check from an unknown donor for the exact amount needed to meet that month's budget.

I have witnessed numerous miraculous healings in response to prayer—from medically verified cases of cancer disappearing to legally blind individuals receiving perfect vision. Beyond physical healing, I've seen prayer restore broken marriages, reconcile church divisions, and bring prodigal children back to their families. Through prayer, I've watched revival break out in congregations and impact entire communities.

These testimonies represent just a fraction of the countless ways I have seen God respond to prayer. They stand as vivid reminders that prayer is not merely a religious exercise—it is the means by which we participate in God's transforming work in the world.

Prayer is critical to the way God gets things done on the earth. Without prayer, most of what God wants to do would never be accomplished. He works on the earth through the agency of man. Generally speaking, if we do not pray it, it will not happen.

4

Things that Nullify Fasting

FASTING IS MORE THAN merely shutting off food intake. Our attitudes, words, and actions need to align with what has already been said about the purpose of fasting. When that alignment is not taking place, the fast can become ineffective. What are the things that can nullify or cancel out the effectiveness of fasting?

1. Desiring to be seen. Fasting should never be motivated by a desire to be perceived as spiritual. Jesus gave this instruction in Matthew 6:16–18:

> "When you fast, do not look somber as the hypocrites do, for they disfigure their faces to show others they are fasting. Truly I tell you, they have received their reward in full. But when you fast, put oil on your head and wash your face, so that it will not be obvious to others that you are fasting, but only to your Father, who is unseen; and your Father, who sees what is done in secret, will reward you."

Try not to make it outwardly obvious that you are fasting. Fasting is a private act of devotion between you and the Father, or between a group of people and their Father.

2. Doing as you please on the day of your fasting. The prophet Isaiah spoke of a people who wondered why their fasting was ineffective. (You can read about this in Isaiah 58.) These people said, "Why have we fasted,... and you have not seen it? Why have we humbled ourselves, and you have not noticed?" He responded by drawing their attention to the fact that on the day of their fasting, they were doing as *they* pleased.

The prophet Jeremiah gave a similar message in Jeremiah 14:10–12: "They greatly love to wander; they do not restrain their feet. So the Lord does not accept them.... Although they fast, I will not listen to their cry." When people have no intention to forsake their love for wandering or restrain their undisciplined ways, their fasting is wasted.

During a fast, the attitude of the heart should be to bring all personal desires into submission to what *God* desires. Fasting is a time for habits and routines to be transformed, not to remain unchanged.

3. Exploiting people who serve or work for you. The prophet Isaiah gave this rebuke: "On the day of your fasting, you do as you please and exploit all your workers" (Isaiah 58:3). If you are a person who has supervisory authority over others, your season of fasting is a time to remind yourself to be kind to them. Any pattern of taking undue advantage of them must be broken.

During your fast, perhaps it would be a good idea to surprise those who serve you with a generous act of kindness. Better yet, implement a new routine of kindness that you will sustain beyond the fast. Obviously, there is a principle here that applies to the way employers treat their employees, but it is also applicable to the way we treat the person who mows our lawn, the hairdresser who cuts our hair, or the server who waits on us at the restaurant. Let us also consider how members of our own household may need to be treated more kindly.

4. Participation in quarreling, strife, accusation, and malicious talk. Adversarial words and conduct are unbecoming of a Christian, and they negate the effectiveness of a fast. Once again, it is the prophet Isaiah who addresses this issue, saying, "Your fasting ends in quarreling and strife, and in striking each other with wicked fists. You cannot fast as you do today and expect your voice to be heard on high" (Isaiah 58:4). Without immediate confession and repentance, one may be better off breaking the fast and starting over at a later time.

5. Neglecting the needy. As suggested elsewhere in our study, fasting should not be a self-oriented practice. When we fast, we empty ourselves, and when we empty ourselves, we are then in a better condition to serve others. When we are full of ourselves, we serve ourselves. After we press through the initial phase of a fast, when our flesh cries out to be fed, we reach a point where we become less aware of ourselves. At that point, we should intentionally consider the needs of others. If the needs of others become apparent to us, and we continue to neglect them, then we are negating the potential benefit of the fast. Consider the words of the Lord through the prophet Isaiah:

> "Is not this the kind of fasting I have chosen: to loose the chains of injustice and untie the cords of the yoke, to set the oppressed free and break every yoke? Is it not to share your food with the hungry and to provide the poor wanderer with shelter—when you see the naked, to clothe them, and not to turn away from your own flesh and blood?" (Isaiah 58:6–7).

If we allow ourselves to become more aware of human needs during our fasts, and if we respond with acts of benevolence and justice, great promise accompanies us. Consider the word of the Lord to those who act to correct injustice:

> Then your light will break forth like the dawn, and your healing will quickly appear; then your righteousness will go before you, and the glory of the Lord will be your rear guard. Then you will call, and the Lord will answer; you will cry for help, and he will say: "Here am I."
>
> If you do away with the yoke of oppression, with the pointing finger and malicious talk, and if you spend yourselves in behalf of the hungry and satisfy the needs of the oppressed, then your light will rise in the darkness, and your night will become like the noonday. The Lord will guide you always; he will satisfy your needs in a sun-scorched land and will strengthen your frame. You will be like a well-watered garden, like a spring whose waters never fail (Isaiah 58:8–11).

Based on this passage, these are God's promises to those whose fasting is accompanied by care for the needy and the oppressed: accelerated healing, answered prayer, the satisfying of personal needs, strength, prosperity, divine protection, and guidance.

5

How to Fast

FASTING DOES NOT COME naturally. The natural inclination of the human body is to eat, not to refrain from eating. To enter into this discipline, believers need God's empowering grace, and they need someone to teach them. The teaching may come in the form of an example set by a leader living a lifestyle of prayer and fasting, or a personal mentor may offer the needed instruction. The teaching may also be presented through sermons, lectures, or reading materials, such as this book.

Before exploring how to fast, it's important to understand the different types of fasting available to us. Then, with this foundation, we can better implement the practical guidelines that follow.

Types of Fasting

Understanding different types of fasting can help you discern which approach the Lord may be leading you to take. While the Bible presents various examples of fasting, several common patterns have emerged through church history and practice:

Complete Fast

This type of fast involves abstaining from all food and drinking only water. Jesus conducted this type of fast during his forty days in the wilderness. A complete fast requires careful preparation and should not be undertaken for extended periods without spiritual and medical guidance. Some choose to observe complete fasts for shorter durations, such as one to three days.

Juice Fast

During a juice fast, individuals abstain from solid foods while drinking fruit and vegetable juices. This approach provides some nutritional support while still maintaining the discipline of denying physical hunger. When juice fasting, it's advisable to dilute fruit juices to moderate sugar intake and reduce the potential adverse effect of acids found in fruits. It is advisable to include vegetable juices for balanced nutrition.

Daniel Fast

Based on Daniel's experience recorded in Daniel 1, this partial fast restricts diet to vegetables, fruits, and water, eliminating meats, sweets, and other rich foods. Generally, if it comes from seed, you can eat it. In Daniel 10, we see another example where Daniel abstained from "choice food," meat, and wine. The Daniel fast has become particularly popular for extended fasts because it allows adequate nutrition while still requiring significant dietary discipline.

Partial Fast

This approach involves giving up specific foods or meals. Some choose to skip particular meals each day while maintaining normal eating at other times. Others may eliminate specific food categories (such as sweets or meat) for the duration of their fast. Partial fasts can be especially appropriate for those who cannot safely undertake a complete fast due to health conditions or work requirements.

Supernatural Fast

While rare, Scripture records instances where God supernaturally sustained individuals during extended fasts, as with Moses on Mount Sinai (Exodus 34:28) and Elijah's journey to Horeb (1 Kings 19:8). We should not presume upon such supernatural provision but rather seek the Lord's specific direction for our fasting.

Non-Food Fasts

There are times when the Lord may lead you to fast from things other than food. This approach is addressed elsewhere in this book. It might include abstaining from entertainment, social media, shopping, or other activities that normally occupy your time and attention. Such fasts can be particularly meaningful when they create space for prayer and seeking God's face.

The key is not which type of fast you choose, but rather that your choice aligns with the Holy Spirit's leading and your current circumstances. Some considerations in choosing the type of fast include:

- Your current health condition

- Your work and family responsibilities

- The duration of the fast

- Your level of experience with fasting

- The specific purpose for which you are fasting

Remember that the power of fasting lies not in its particular form but in the heart attitude of humbling oneself before God. Whether he leads you to undertake a complete fast or a partial restriction of food or activities, the goal remains the same: drawing closer to him and positioning yourself to receive what he wants to do in and through your life.

Practical Guidelines

Now that we understand the various approaches to fasting, let's examine how to implement them effectively. The following instructions have been drafted for the twenty-one-day fast, but they should also prove helpful for fasts of any length.

1. Wisely schedule your fast. It is not typically a good idea to schedule a fast for times when feasting should be taking place. Do you realize that feasting is just as biblical as fasting? You may want to consider not fasting at a time when you should be enjoying major holidays, a family member's birthday party, or a friend's wedding reception. Even when scheduling a twenty-one-day fast at the beginning of a year, starting the fast one or two days after New Year's Day may be advisable.

2. Assess your physical readiness for the fast. Please consult with your physician before pursuing an extended fast, especially if you are already dealing with serious health issues. Some people are not able to fast for medical reasons. In such cases, I would encourage those individuals to ask the Lord, "What can I give up during this fast that I might otherwise enjoy?"

If you are physically fit and have a regular exercise routine, do your best to maintain a reasonable amount of exercise. If you attempt an extended fast without including exercise, you might experience muscle tissue loss. It may be a good idea to start an exercise routine several weeks before a fast and sustain it throughout the fast.

3. Ask God how you should conduct your fast. Ask the Lord how many days or how many meals he wants you to fast. Also, ask the Lord to what degree you should fast. For instance, at times, one may want to fast solid food but continue to take in fruit and vegetable juices. Once you ask him, pay attention to the wisdom that starts coming to your mind. If your fasting is in obedience to God's wisdom and instruction, then you will have the grace to sustain the fast.

4. Submit to the leading of the Holy Spirit. When Jesus started his forty-day fast, the Holy Spirit compelled him to enter a wilderness. Let the Holy Spirit drive you into the "wilderness" to fast. The wilderness is not just a desert. There is life in the wilderness—that set apart place free from life's normal routines and distractions. The wilderness is where God is. There are many biblical examples to establish this truth.

5. Prepare for the fast. In the days leading up to the fast, fine-tune your prayer life and Bible reading habits. Rearrange your calendar and daily schedule to create space for more time with the Lord. Be sure to adjust your eating habits as well. If you drink coffee, it is a good idea to taper off before the fast begins.

6. Start with a shorter fast. If you have never fasted before, start with a meal or a day. Those accustomed to short fasts might want to consider going on a longer fast.

7. Step out with confidence. Fasting is a venture of faith, and God is faithful to meet us when we take the "risk" to trust him. As you get to know him better, you will find that steps of faith are never really a risk; he is always faithful. As you fast, know that the Holy Spirit will sustain you.

8. For extended fasts, taper in and taper out. By all means, do not stuff yourself with food the day before the fast begins! The same applies for when the fast has been completed. Gradually taper out of extended fasts with an intake of liquids.

9. For extended fasts, drink fluids. Water should be your primary fluid. Some fruit juice or vegetable juice might be advisable on extended fasts; it is all up to you and the Lord to make those decisions. If you decide to drink fruit juices, acidic juices may need to be watered down. As far as drinking milk is concerned, understand that milk is about the most perfect source of nourishment that God created; therefore, satisfying hunger by drinking milk on a fast practically nullifies the effect of the fast.

10. Conduct your fast with joy. Be worshipful, and maintain a joyful countenance and appearance throughout the fast. Jesus taught us, saying,

> "When you fast, do not look somber as the hypocrites do, for they disfigure their faces to show others they are fasting. Truly I tell you, they have received their reward in full. But when you fast, put oil on your head and wash your face, so that it will not be obvious to others that you are fasting, but only to your Father, who is unseen; and your Father, who sees what is done in secret, will reward you" (Matthew 6:16–18).

11. Don't talk about it much. In light of what we just read in Matthew 6, your fast should remain private. Of course, you should tell your immediate family members so that they will understand why you are not coming to the dinner table. If you find yourself in a situation where you must join others for a meal, it is not typically awkward to refrain from eating. As long as you are normally engaged in conversation, people will hardly notice that you are not eating.

12. Sustain yourself with spiritual food. When you fast, you intentionally create a void in your life to make more room for God and the things of God. When you draw aside and away from others for prayer, Bible reading, and reflection, you fill that void with the Lord's presence. I consider such times as "feasting while I'm fasting."

13. Lay aside things that might distract from prayer, Bible reading, and intimate communion with the Lord. For some, this time of consecration may mean eliminating television and social media. For all, it should involve eliminating negative speaking and thinking, as Steve and Wendy Backlund teach in their material on negativity fasts. Ask the Father, "How should I upgrade my prayer life during this fast? How should I improve my Bible reading and my times of meditation?"

14. Look for opportunities to become outwardly focused during your fast. In your fasting, you are dying to yourself. You are becoming less concerned about yourself and more concerned about the glory of God and the well-being of others. In the chapter "Things that Nullify Fasting," we have already noted the power of an outward focus, as seen in Isaiah 58. Becoming outwardly focused is a key to breakthrough and one of the most significant aspects of becoming Christlike.

15. Don't be surprised if the fast becomes both physically and spiritually challenging. Fasting is, in many ways, a self-imposed wilderness experience. It is, in fact, an act of offensive spiritual warfare. You may face spiritual resistance while you are fasting. Be aware that it is in such times that our faults can surface. Remember that the "breakthrough" does not usually come until the fast ends. Jesus' forty days in the wilderness is a good example (Matthew 4:1–11). Temptations bombarded Jesus during his fast, but when the fast had concluded, the blessing came: angels came and ministered to him.

16. Learn how to deal with food cravings. While fasting, fleeting thoughts of your favorite things to eat may momentarily come upon you. If you cannot seem to discard the thought and it becomes a distraction, try writing it down. Keep a notepad on hand for this purpose. You can postpone the thought or desire by making a list of meals and food items you are craving. When you write it down, you tell yourself, "I can think about this another time."

17. If you yield to the temptation to eat, do not give up. If you get three days into a fast and eat a cookie, a potato chip, or even an entire meal, have you ended your fast? It depends on what you decide to do at that point. You can end it if you want to. You are under no legalistic obligation to continue. However, you can also choose to resume your fast. If you feel you should complete the fast, give yourself grace, and continue.

18. If you decide to end your fast earlier than planned, celebrate your gains. Even if you cut your fast short, whatever you have devoted to the Lord is pleasing in his eyes. The progress you have made does not get canceled out just because your fast has ended sooner than expected.

Fasting in Family Life

Fasting while managing family responsibilities presents unique challenges, especially when other family members are not participating in the fast.

How do we maintain our spiritual discipline while fulfilling our roles as parents, spouses, and caregivers?

When Other Family Members Aren't Fasting

The decision to fast is deeply personal, and we should never pressure family members to join us. When you are the only one fasting in your household, maintain a spirit of grace and avoid drawing attention to your sacrifice. Continue to prepare meals for your family with love and care. Some find it helpful to prepare meals in advance or simplify meal preparation during their fast to minimize time handling food.

Remember that your fast should not become a source of tension in your home. If your spouse or children ask why you're not eating, respond with gentleness and brevity. Your fast should draw you closer to both God and your family, not create distance between you.

Fasting as a Parent

Parents of young children face particular challenges while fasting. The demands of childcare require energy and attention, making extended fasts especially challenging. Consider these practical approaches:

Consider timing your extended prayer periods during children's nap times or after bedtime. Early morning prayer before the household awakens can provide uninterrupted time with the Lord. If possible, arrange with your spouse or a trusted friend to watch the children for short periods so you can focus on prayer.

When fasting while caring for children, be attentive to your energy levels and adjust your fast as needed. There's no shame in modifying your fast to ensure you can properly care for your little ones. Some parents find success with partial fasts or shortened fasting periods that allow them to maintain the strength needed for childcare.

Family mealtimes present special challenges during a fast. Rather than avoiding family meals, use this time to focus on nurturing family relationships. Engage in conversation, listen to your children's stories, and demonstrate that fellowship matters more than food. This models for children that our spiritual lives integrate naturally with family life.

If you have older children, your fast might prompt questions about spiritual disciplines. Use these moments as opportunities for age-appropriate teaching about seeking God. Instead of focusing on the mechanics of fasting, share stories of answered prayers and God's faithfulness.

Remember that your role as a parent is itself a sacred calling. Sometimes, the most spiritual thing you can do while fasting is to remain fully present and patient with your children. Your fast should enhance, not diminish, your ability to reflect God's love to your family.

For parents of infants or nursing mothers, traditional food fasts may not be advisable. Consider other forms of fasting that don't compromise your ability to care for and nurture your child. The Lord understands the seasons of life and honors your heart's desire to seek him while fulfilling your parental responsibilities.

Fasting in Modern Work Environments

The modern workplace—whether remote, hybrid, or in-office—presents unique challenges and opportunities for fasting individuals. Successfully maintaining a fast while fulfilling professional responsibilities requires thoughtful planning and discretion.

For those working remotely, create a dedicated prayer space separate from your work area to help maintain clear boundaries between work and spiritual disciplines. The time previously spent commuting can be redirected to prayer and Bible reading. Short prayer breaks can help maintain spiritual focus throughout the day between virtual meetings. Many find it beneficial to turn off notifications during designated prayer times, and lunch breaks can become valuable windows for prayer rather than browsing social media or catching up on work.

In traditional office settings, consider reserving a conference room or finding a quiet space for prayer during breaks. A small Bible or devotional on your desk can provide brief moments of spiritual refreshment throughout the day. Some find that taking prayer walks near their workplace helps them stay connected to God while managing workplace demands. If other believers in your workplace are fasting, connecting with them can provide valuable mutual support.

Meetings and meals present particular challenges during a fast. Try to schedule important meetings outside typical meal times. You can attend unavoidable lunch meetings while drinking water or taking notes. During team celebrations or office parties, focus on building relationships rather than food. When asked about not eating, a simple response like "I'm taking a break from lunch today" usually satisfies curiosity without drawing unnecessary attention to your fast.

Energy and focus management become especially important while fasting at work. Consider scheduling challenging tasks during peak energy hours, taking short walks to refresh your mind and spirit, and keeping water nearby to stay hydrated. Pay attention to your energy levels and adjust your workload when possible.

Establishing clear boundaries helps protect fasting time in our digitally connected workplaces. Rather than constantly monitoring email, set specific times to check it. Minimize digital distractions during dedicated prayer times. After work hours, consider implementing a "digital sunset" to create space for evening prayer and reflection.

The key is to approach workplace fasting with wisdom and discretion. Remember that fasting is about deepening your relationship with God, not proving anything to colleagues. With thoughtful planning, you can maintain your professional responsibilities and spiritual discipline while maintaining the private nature of your fast.

Fasting, Mental Health, and Stress Management

While fasting can bring profound spiritual benefits, we must approach it with wisdom regarding our mental and emotional well-being. Physical fasting can temporarily affect mood, concentration, and emotional resilience. These effects are typical and often part of the process that leads us to greater dependence on God. However, individuals managing anxiety, depression, or other mental health conditions should take particular care when approaching a fast. In these situations, it is important to consult both medical advisors and spiritual mentors before beginning a fast.

The connection between body and mind during a fast can work in our favor when we approach it with understanding and preparation. Many find that fasting, when done correctly, actually helps reduce anxiety and mental clutter. As we release our usual patterns of consumption, we often experience a settling of mental chaos and a quieting of racing thoughts. This mental clarity can enhance our ability to hear God's voice and receive his peace.

Some people discover that fasting unveils emotional patterns they hadn't previously recognized. When we remove food as a coping mechanism, we might become more aware of how we use eating to manage stress or emotional discomfort. While potentially challenging, this awareness creates opportunities for deeper healing and the development of healthier spiritual coping strategies.

If you are dealing with high stress levels, rather than viewing fasting as another demand on your already stretched resources, see it as an invitation to release burdens to the Lord. Jesus's words take on special meaning here: "Come to me, all you who are weary and burdened, and I will give you rest" (Matthew 11:28). Fasting becomes an act of trust, saying, "Lord, I'm laying down my normal ways of coping and choosing to depend entirely on you."

If you find yourself struggling with anxiety or depression during a fast, remember that modifying or ending the fast is not failure. God's grace is sufficient, and he honors our sincere efforts to seek him, even when those efforts look different than what we initially planned.

Those with a history of eating disorders or related mental health challenges should be particularly cautious about food-based fasts. Alternative forms of fasting are discussed elsewhere in this book, and they might be more appropriate and spiritually beneficial.

The goal is to foster a healthy relationship with God and self, not to create additional mental or emotional strain. If mental health challenges arise during your fast, bring them to the Lord in prayer. He often uses these moments of vulnerability to reveal his tender care for every aspect of our well-being—body, mind, and spirit.

6

Congregational Implementation

THE CONGREGATIONAL CALL TO a twenty-one-day season of prayer and fasting does not necessarily mean that everyone is expected to live on a water-only diet for three weeks. Rather, it is a twenty-one-day period in which the church engages in a corporate emphasis on fasting and prayer. It is each individual's responsibility to voluntarily decide the level of personal participation.

This chapter offers several practical resources for the implementation of the twenty-one day prayer and fasting emphasis:

- A timeline and checklist for preparations and implementation

- A sample letter from the pastor

- Guidelines for personal prayer sessions

- Guidelines for group prayer sessions

- Guidelines for conducting a solemn assembly

Timeline and Checklist

The following is a suggested timeline and checklist.

1. _____ The pastor or leader establishes a consistent discipline of prayer and fasting in his or her own life.

2. _____ Recruit key intercessors and leaders to assist in planning and implementing the fast.

3. _____ Set up the church calendar to accommodate the twenty-one-day corporate fast.

4. _____ Decide what portions of the prayer time will be conducted in group settings and what portions will be conducted privately on an individual basis.

5. _____ Teach and preach on prayer and fasting.

6. _____ Schedule public testimonies from people who have experienced breakthroughs in prayer and fasting.

7. _____ Prepare for the distribution of a schedule and a concise list of guidelines.

8. _____ Before the scheduled fast, repeatedly announce and promote the prayer and fasting emphasis through social media, emails, public announcements, posters, bulletin inserts, mailings, etc.

9. _____ Order printed copies of this book, *21 Days of Prayer and*

Fasting (second edition), making it available to the congregation.

10. _____ Make supplemental materials related to prayer and fasting available to the group. Richard Foster's *Celebration of Discipline* is a good resource, and the author's book *101 Prayer Models* may also prove helpful.

11. _____ First Sign-up Sunday: Set up a sign-up table in the church's foyer, using a sign-up sheet on which participants indicate the days they will be participating in the twenty-one-day period. If the preference is to keep the sign-up anonymous, individuals can place a checkmark on the days of their choice.

12. _____ Second Sign-up Sunday: Repeat the procedure noted for the first sign-up Sunday.

13. _____ Day 1: Conduct a Solemn Assembly. Lead individuals, families, and the church through repentance, forgiveness, and cleansing.

14. _____ Days 2 through 20: Conduct a series of group prayer times at the church, in homes, or in other designated places.

15. _____ Days 2 through 20: Throughout this period, the pastor or leader should publicly encourage the group in the prayer and fasting project each time they gather.

16. _____ Day 21: Conduct a Communion Service to close out the 21 days. Announce a scheduled Celebration event. This event is a time for the group to celebrate and bring closure to the group's prayer and fasting emphasis.

17. _____ Conduct the Celebration event. Share a light meal together, and invite testimonies.

18. _____ Continue prayer and fasting as an ongoing part of the group's corporate life.

Sample Letter from the Pastor

The following sample letter can be used for a January prayer and fasting emphasis. It may also be modified for use at other times of the year.

Dear Friends,

Thank you for agreeing to join us for these twenty-one days of prayer and fasting. The fast begins <START DATE> and ends <END DATE>.

We are not necessarily asking you as an individual to fast the entire span of twenty-one days. Ask the Lord what portion of these twenty-one days he would have you participate. Together as a body, we will fulfill the call to a corporate fast.

Why are we calling this fast? As we enter a new ministry year, we each need to consecrate ourselves to the Lord. We want to be cleansed of any hindrances we have picked up along the way, so we ask the Lord to search our hearts and cause us to repent of whatever sins he may bring to our awareness. We want to bring ourselves into complete submission to his will. This is also a time to learn to hear his voice and to be revived in our passion for Jesus.

In addition to personal consecration, this fast is a time to intercede. Let us pray for our own families, church families, church leaders, pastoral team, and church staff, as well as our community, neighbors, friends, associates, the surrounding region, state, nation, and the world. Let us pray for revival and the harvest of souls.

The church will be open for additional hours of prayer in addition to its regular worship service times. A schedule is enclosed with this letter.

If you need encouragement or further guidance during this fast, please feel free to call upon one of the church's elders. Printed guidelines and support materials are also available in the church foyer.

I am looking forward to taking this journey together!

Sincerely,

<LEADER'S NAME>

Guidelines for Personal Prayer Sessions

Some people find it easier to pray with groups of people. Others are more comfortable praying alone. It is important to learn to pray in both modes.

Jesus is our example in everything. There were times that he prayed alone, and there were times when he prayed with others joining him. Here, we will note guidelines for personal prayer times, and later, we will cover how to conduct group prayer sessions.

1. Schedule a daily time for prayer.

2. Prepare a set-apart place where you will pray daily—a place free from distractions.

3. Take water with you into your prayer time.

4. Take your Bible with you into your prayer time. Bible reading may be included either before or after prayer. As you pray, you may also need your Bible for those moments when the Holy Spirit draws your thoughts to particular passages.

5. Take a journal and notepad with you into your prayer time. The journal is for writing down reflections and insights the Lord may impress upon you. It is also a good place to keep your prayer list and to record testimonies of answered prayer. The notepad is for jotting down distracting thoughts of things you need to do. By jotting them down, you can postpone those thoughts for later.

6. Silence and put aside your electronic devices.

7. You may want to take communion elements (grape juice and bread) into your prayer time.

8. To assist with staying focused in prayer, try changing postures. You may want to sit, kneel, or pace. If you are in a time of soaking

prayer, you can lie down.

9. Consider playing recorded *instrumental* music while you are praying. While music with appropriate lyrics can be helpful, it may sometimes carry your thoughts in the direction of the lyrics and distract your praying.

10. Make yourself aware of God's presence by turning your affections toward him.

11. "Soak" in his presence, and meditate on his goodness.

12. Start your praying with thanksgiving, adoration, worship, and praise.

13. Pray for yourself and your household.

14. Pray for others.

15. End your praying with thanksgiving, adoration, worship, and praise.

Guidelines for Group Prayer Sessions

When workers arrive at a construction site, they expect to find a blueprint and guidance for the project. They have not been employed just to erect any kind of building. They have not come to construct whatever each of them individually feels like constructing. They have been employed as a crew to work together to erect one particular building with specifications unique to its function. The blueprint is a reference for them, and the supervisor will direct their work. If they follow the blueprint and the guidance of their supervisor, the result will be an edifice completed according to the plan.

The same is true of group prayer sessions. When pray-ers arrive at a prayer meeting, they expect to find a plan and guidance for the prayer meeting. Planning is needed. They have not come just to pray; they could do that at home. They have come together as a prayer team desiring a God-ordained purpose. Someone needs to pray prior to the prayer meeting to ask heaven for a blueprint. That person should then facilitate the movement of the group through their prayer session. If the group follows the facilitator's blueprint and guidance, they are more likely to fulfill their prayer assignment with a sense of accomplishment. Advanced spirit-led planning is a key to successful group prayer sessions.

Planning for prayer meetings should include the following:

1. Praying for the prayer gathering and its prospective participants, asking God for the plan or blueprint.

2. Identifying a time and a place to gather.

3. Identifying and orienting members of the leadership and facilitation team.

4. Preparing an outline or format for the gathering, including a sequence of movements or events to take place in the session.

5. Communicating to prospective participants essential information about the time, place and purpose of the gathering.

6. Acquiring and preparing the resources needed for the gathering, such as prayer guides, notepads, water, music (live or record-

ed), communion elements, prayer cloths, anointing oil, banners, maps, fruit for those who may not be on a total fast and other support materials.

7. Prayer over the physical space in which the praying will take place. (What an added blessing it is when pray-ers arrive and discover that the environment is already permeated with the manifest presence of God.)

While facilitators of prayer groups can expect the Holy Spirit to guide them in their planning, following the example of how others have conducted prayer meetings may prove helpful. The following format serves as an example:

1. Open with prayer. In the opening prayer, pray for protection over those who are assembled and their family members at home. Pray that every backlash planned by the enemy will fail. Pray for wisdom in the flow and direction of the praying. Pray for God's presence to be manifested, so that the praying will take place from a place of his presence.

It is also a good idea to give participants an opportunity to unload any personal burdens that could distract them during their prayer time. Invite them to pair off with someone to share whatever needs may be on their minds. By praying over one another, those needs are quickly taken to the Lord, freeing them to pray for others as the prayer session progresses.

2. Worship and listen. Through thanksgiving, worship, and praise, participants are given the opportunity to become aware of God's presence. In his presence, his heart and will can be discerned. Encourage the people to listen as they worship. At such times, prophetic guidance often comes to those who have gathered to pray. As pray-ers listen, they allow the Holy Spirit to prepare the list of things to pray about.

3. Share and discern. Once participants have heard from the Lord, they may share what they have heard. If a large number of people have gathered, the group may need to be divided into smaller groups. In small groups, the people can share what they believe God is saying, and authorized group facilitators can then discern whether or not those insights benefit the direction of the prayer session.

4. Pray. Once again, divide into groups. The person designated as the leader of the prayer gathering will decide how the groups will be constituted. A leader should be assigned to each group. Leaders will not dominate the praying; they are merely facilitators. The leader will appropriately direct the group in praying over the matters that the Holy Spirit has already highlighted.

In some faith traditions, it is appropriate for everyone to pray aloud simultaneously. However, in this group prayer model, participants need to be more inclined to listen than to speak. Participants typically speak one at a time, and as each speaks, the rest pray in agreement with what is being said.

Initial statements in prayer should be words of worship and praise. We do not need to make speeches to the group during our prayers. Group prayer is not the time to inform the group or promote personal agendas. We should make relatively short statements in prayer, realizing that the Lord may also give other people things to pray about. Lengthy intercession should be reserved for our individual prayer closets.

Do not move too quickly through the prayer list. Wait to move on to another topic until the group has prayed through the previous topic. A prolonged silence could indicate that moving on to the next topic is okay.

It is important that no individual dominate or monopolize the prayer session. If you realize that you have been doing a great deal of the vocal praying, refraining from speaking for a while may be helpful. In this way, you can prefer others above yourself.

While prophetic utterances should be welcomed and encouraged in group prayer settings, we must remember that such words are always subject to the group's discernment, as Paul instructs in 1 Corinthians 14:29–33. When it comes to charismatic gifts, it's essential to honor and follow the theological understanding and practices of the host church or gathering. If you plan to host meetings where prophetic ministry is encouraged regularly, consider providing training in New Testament prophetic ministry. This equips participants to exercise these gifts with wisdom, understanding, and proper biblical foundation.

5. Worship and give thanks. As the prayer session draws to a close, provide time to worship and express gratitude to God for what he has done. If individuals feel that they have had some degree of breakthrough, they should also be given an opportunity to share testimonies.

Guidelines for Conducting a Solemn Assembly

A Solemn Assembly is a sacred time when the entire congregation gathers for focused prayer, repentance, and seeking God's face. Throughout Scripture, God's people assembled solemnly in times of spiritual renewal, crisis, or significant transition. These gatherings require careful preparation and spiritual sensitivity to ensure they fulfill their holy purpose.

1. Prepare the leadership team through prayer and fasting before announcing the Solemn Assembly to the congregation.

2. Choose a date and time that allows the congregation to participate fully. Consider scheduling the assembly on a Saturday morning or

a designated evening when most congregants can attend.

3. Communicate the purpose and significance of the Solemn Assembly to the congregation at least two weeks in advance. Include biblical examples and clear explanations of what to expect.

4. Request that participants prepare their hearts through personal prayer and, if possible, fasting in the days leading up to the assembly.

5. Prepare the sanctuary or meeting space appropriately. Remove any potential distractions and consider arrangements that facilitate both corporate and small-group prayer times.

6. Designate prayer leaders to guide different segments of the assembly. These leaders should be spiritually mature and sensitive to the Holy Spirit's guidance.

7. Structure the assembly to include these essential elements:

   a. *Opening corporate worship*
   b. *Times of silent personal reflection and repentance*
   c. *Corporate prayer and intercession*
   d. *Prophetic ministry as the Spirit leads*
   e. *Communion*
   f. *Declaration of Scripture*
   g. *Closing worship and dedication*

8. Plan for multiple prayer focuses, which may include:

   a. *Personal and corporate repentance*

b. Family restoration
   c. Church unity and renewal
   d. Community transformation
   e. National concerns
   f. Global missions and revival

9. Make provision for those who need individual prayer ministry during the assembly by having designated prayer teams available.

10. Include times of silent waiting on the Lord. These moments allow the Holy Spirit to speak to hearts and guide the assembly's flow.

11. Provide paper and pens for participants to write personal commitments, prayer burdens, or prophetic insights as the Lord leads.

12. Consider incorporating symbolic acts of commitment or consecration, such as:

    a. Anointing with oil for consecration
    b. Foot washing as an act of humility and service
    c. Burning written prayers of renunciation

    Prayers of renunciation involve participants writing down personal sins and burning the papers as a symbol of God's cleansing and forgiveness. Alternative approaches include shredding the pieces of paper or nailing them to a large wooden cross. (This exercise should be conducted in a controlled, reverent manner with appropriate safety measures.)

13. Document significant prophetic words, visions, or corporate

commitments that emerge during the assembly for future reference and follow-up.

14. Plan for appropriate follow-up gatherings or prayer meetings to steward the spiritual momentum generated during the Solemn Assembly.

15. End the assembly with a time of celebration and thanksgiving, acknowledging God's faithfulness and presence throughout the gathering.

Conclusion

No one is really an *expert* in the disciplines of prayer and fasting. There is always more to learn. It is not that these practices are complicated. Rather, the point is that we are on a grand adventure in which the quest for knowing God and his ways is unending. We never reach the point where we can say we have finally arrived. For this reason, we are always to have a teachable and humble spirit. Let us *receive* insight from one another and *give* affirmation to others as they learn and become acclimated to a culture of prayer and fasting.

The thoughts shared in this book should not be perceived as laws or legalistic expectations. We pray and fast because we delight in the Lord, not because he demands it of us. Fasting is a grace-based practice. It is not about us producing more or trying harder. It is the place where we come to the end of our works and arrive at the beginning of His. Striving ceases. Receiving begins. In our weakness, we trust him more.

Let us enter our times of prayer and fasting knowing that willfully becoming weak is a powerful and effective act. The sincere offering of our lives to the Lord is never a wasted sacrifice. To come before him in humility is to encounter his favor. May we proceed confidently knowing that "the prayer of a righteous person is powerful and effective" (James 5:16).

Remember God's promises to those who pray and fast with an upright heart. You cannot engage in these disciplines and remain the same. You will change.

From here to the end of this text, I want to speak prophetically to my readers. (These words are based on James 4, verses 6 and 10, and Isaiah 58.)

In this process, you will become humble, and from that place of humility, God will promote you. You will gain unusual favor. Your prayers will become more effective. Healing and restoration will come quickly. In the moment that you pray, heaven will move in response, even as you are still speaking. As you speak, listen for the Father's answer. He has something to say. May you hear the sound of his voice and know his heart.

Your confidence in the Lord will be sure. He goes before you to prepare the way and walks behind you as your Protector. Darkness will be dispelled. Uncertain paths will be made clear before you. The Lord will guide you, he will fulfill your needs, and he will give you strength. You will emerge from the hidden place of prayer and fasting as "a well-watered garden, like a spring whose waters never fail."

Now, you have been instructed in the basics. You are ready. God's favor awaits you. His empowering grace accompanies you. Nothing can hold you back. Let the journey begin.

21-Day Journal

This journal section has been provided as space to document your insights, prayers, and experiences as you undertake this spiritual journey. I encourage you to use these pages to record what God reveals to you during your season of prayer and fasting.

Your journal can include:

- Scripture insights and revelations
- Personal prayers and conversations with God
- Records of answered prayers
- Prophetic impressions and spiritual insights
- Questions and concerns that arise during your fast
- Physical and spiritual challenges encountered
- Lessons learned about yourself and God
- Dreams or visions that seem spiritually significant
- Areas where you sense God bringing transformation

- Testimonies of breakthrough and victory

Consider dating each entry. This creates a timeline of your journey and helps you track God's faithfulness over these twenty-one days. Feel free to write honestly about challenges or struggles, but prayerfully conclude such entries with expressions of faith, hope, or trust in God's faithfulness. This practice helps maintain a redemptive perspective even in difficult moments.

Journaling itself can become a spiritual discipline—a sacred conversation between you and God. Don't feel pressured to write lengthy entries; sometimes a single verse or brief insight can be profound. The goal isn't to fill pages but to document your journey of drawing closer to God through prayer and fasting.

You may find it valuable to revisit these journal entries in the future, remembering God's faithfulness and the insights gained during this consecrated season.

Day 1

Day 2

Day 3

Day 4

Day 5

Day 6

Day 7

Day 8

Day 9

Day 10

Day 11

Day 12

Day 13

Day 14

Day 15

Day 16

Day 17

Day 18

Day 19

Day 20

Day 21

www.ingramcontent.com/pod-product-compliance
Lightning Source LLC
Chambersburg PA
CBHW061332040426
42444CB00011B/2882